BASIC ESSENTIALS™
CANOE
PADDLING

Help Us Keep This Guide Up to Date

Every effort has been made by the author and editors to make this guide as accurate and useful as possible. However, many things can change after a guide is published—new products and information become available, regulations change, techniques evolve, etc.

We would love to hear from you concerning your experiences with this guide and how you feel it could be improved and be kept up to date. While we may not be able to respond to all comments and suggestions, we'll take them to heart and we'll also make certain to share them with the author. Please send your comments and suggestions to the following address:

The Globe Pequot Press
Reader Response/Editorial Department
P.O. Box 480
Guilford, CT 06437

Or you may e-mail us at:

editorial@globe-pequot.com

Thanks for your input.

BASIC ESSENTIALS™ SERIES

BASIC ✹ ESSENTIALS™

CANOE PADDLING

SECOND EDITION

BY HARRY ROBERTS

REVISED AND EDITED BY STEVE SALINS

The Globe Pequot Press

Guilford, Connecticut

Cover photo © Gary McGuffin
Cover design by Lana Mullen
Text and layout design by Casey Shain
Illustrations by Bev Rich

Library of Congress Cataloging-in-Publication Data

Roberts, Harry.
  Basic essentials : Canoe Paddling / by Harry Roberts. — 2nd ed. / revised and edited by Steve Salins.
       p. cm. — (Basic essentials series)
     Rev. ed. of: The basic essentials of canoe paddling. c1992.
     Includes index.
     ISBN: 0-7627-0662-7
     1. Canoes and canoeing.   I. Title: Canoe paddling. II. Salins, Steve. III. Roberts, Harry. Basic essentials: canoe paddling.
  GV783.R6 2000
  797.1'22—DC21   00-021183
                                                              CIP

Manufactured in the United States of America
Second Edition/First Printing

Contents

Introduction

This book is about paddling. It's not about selecting a canoe. It's not about tents or sleeping bags or cooking gear or portage packs. It's about paddling. Because paddling is, in my experience, the part of canoeing that's frequently forgotten, even though it's the part of canoeing that can make or break your trip.

There's a popular notion that anybody can paddle. But let's rephrase that. Anybody can be *taught* to paddle. To paddle well, paddle easily, paddle efficiently, paddle in control, and paddle safely.

But why bother, you ask? Millions of people go canoeing every weekend and seem to be having a good time, and most of them don't paddle well. Why bother?

Well, are you sure they're having a good time? If they were, they'd be out on the water next week; maybe even out on the water the next day, in their own canoe. The fact is that most have a good time swimming, or fishing, or splashing water and tipping over, or, in what's come to be a noxious tradition on many waterways, getting drunk and rowdy. A few enjoy watching birds, sensing the constant variations of light dancing on the water, and slipping into a oneness with the natural world. But very few enjoy paddling. Very few get involved in the feel of a good canoe slipping quickly, easily, and powerfully through the water under perfect and nearly unconscious control. Very few paddle well enough to be free to absorb the world around them without worrying about wind, waves, current, and even a fundamental thing like keeping the boat going straight.

In simple terms, learning to paddle well gives you the skills to enjoy canoeing more. Who knows? You might even find yourself catching an hour on the water every day after dinner! Most of us live close enough to a paddleable waterway to do just that. But you'll never do that unless you enjoy paddling—the art and craft of making a canoe do exactly what you want it to do when you want it to.

So—we'll be talking together about the easiest way to learn to paddle. And I mean *easiest*. This isn't the School of One Thousand Strokes and a Stroke! It's a couple of strokes—but strokes learned so well that you don't have to think about them. And before we start, I'd like to ask you one favor. This is a contemporary approach to paddling. If you've learned a bit about paddling in the past—as I did—you'll be confused by some of what you'll read. You'll be told that it's not only okay to sit in a canoe—you'll be told that it's generally preferable. You probably won't recognize the paddle I'll recommend. And you'll be told that switching sides when you paddle is a sign of artistry, not a sign of terminal ineptitude.

This is a new way to paddle; new at least to a lot of folks. Its fancy name is "North American Touring Technique," and I confess I coined that name for it. Marathon racers—those men and women who paddle long distances in skinny canoes at average speeds of over 7 miles per hour on dead-flat water—call it "sit-and-switch." It's an accurate name. You do sit in the canoe, and you switch sides. You switch sides to aid in directional control, to encourage more efficient strokes, and to distribute the effort among powerful muscle groups. But "sit-and-switch" is an unlovely phrase at best, evoking memories of parental discipline rather than thoughts of clear water and the sound of a canoe running at speed. Clearly, the name needed some gussying up. So—it became North American Touring Technique, or NATT for short.

The name's a mouthful. And I promise I won't use it again until the last chapter in the book. But when you start paddling this way, and you just plain flat-out blow the rails off your companions and get to the takeout so far ahead of them that you were able to read the first half of *Anna Karenina* and still add three birds to your life list, I'd appreciate it if you'd tell your friends the full name for the way you paddle. It'd make me feel good. It really would.

And it'd make me feel good to see the looks of astonishment on the faces of your paddling buddies when you and your partner just take off and leave them, with smiles on your faces and a notable absence of sweat on your brows. I won't be there, of course. But I've seen that look enough to know what it is—and I'm smiling already.

I've run off at the mouth enough. Zip up your PFD and let's go paddling!

BASIC ESSENTIALS

Starting Right

I can only assume you already have a canoe and a partner who's willing to forgive you your trespasses. If you don't, I'd need a book about this size just to talk about the process of selecting a canoe. Yeah, there are that many choices, and designs are subtle. But, as we don't have that other book, I'll have to assume that you own a canoe, and that your primary intent is to take that canoe somewhere and look at something. If you lust for the thrill of playing in whitewater, you've bought the wrong book. If you drool over sea kayaks, you've bought the wrong book. What can I tell you?

Your Paddle

When it's time to go somewhere in a canoe, the paddle you should have to maintain both nice control and efficient paddling is a "bent-shaft" paddle (Figure 1-1) of approximately fifteen degrees. I can hear you now: "Buy another paddle?" Yup—when you're ready to move a canoe, there is no more efficient tool for making it happen than a bent-shaft paddle. What we're talking about here is movement, glide, power, efficiency…cruisin'—what makes paddling fun and draws you out on the water again and again!

Your outfitter should know what you mean when you tell him you want a fifteen-degree bent-shaft, although when you see one you may think it's damaged because there will be an angle between the shaft and the blade.

You probably already have some paddles. If you bought your canoe from a shop, they may have added or sold you some inexpensive paddles. If you got a "pre-paddled" canoe, the previous owner may have included old paddles as incentive for you to pay his asking price. In any case, you more than likely have a couple of straight paddling sticks to get you started. That's okay; we'll talk about using a "straight-shaft" paddle (Figure 1-1) as we go along.

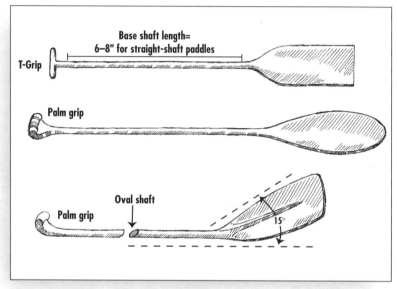

Figure 1-1: Straight- and bent-shaft paddles

Why a bent shaft of about fifteen degrees? Simple. A paddle functions efficiently within a range of fifteen degrees to either side of vertical. Build in the angle to begin with, and you can use a shorter, less tiring stroke with a shorter, lighter, handier paddle. Who wouldn't buy that? I recommend a blade width of no more than 8 inches and a blade length of 18 to 20 inches. Why? A moderately small blade won't twist in your hand under power, and it will be less tiring to paddle. I insist the shaft be oval rather than round so it fits more comfortably in my lower hand and so I know and can control exactly how my blade enters the water. I also want the grip—that knob on the top of the shaft—to be what's generally called a "palm grip." That's because in using this bent-shaft power machine, we push down the shaft and a palm grip is much more comfortable and less tiring for the upper hand.

Now, how do we fit this strange tool (Figure 1-2)? Size is important here; you'd make sure hiking boots fit perfectly and your paddle should fit you no less well. When you go to your outfitter, have them sit you on a flat chair or bench. Turn the paddle upside down, and place the handle between your legs with the shaft vertical. If you're sitting erect, your nose should touch the throat of the paddle—that place on the paddle where blade changes to shaft. That measurement, from bench to nose, is called "Base Shaft Length." I don't know what canoe you're paddling but unless it's a big tripping boat with a flared bow, a bent-shaft paddle with a shaft length of that measurement will do you nicely. If you paddle a big tripper, one that's 25 inches wide or more from rail to rail at the bow seat, consider a stick with a shaft length 1 or 2 inches longer.

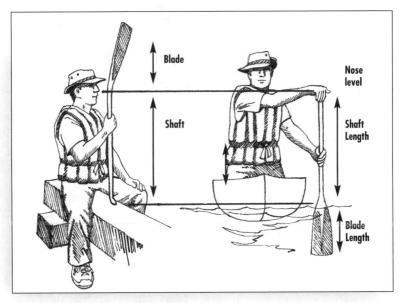

Figure 1-2: Sizing a bent-shaft paddle

If in spite of my open, honest manner and reputation for trust-worthiness you prefer a straight-shaft paddle because some guru told you to use one for better canoe control, add 6 to 8 inches to that base shaft length for your straight-shaft paddle. (Maybe you'd better bring those paddles you got with the canoe along with you to the outfitter—just in case you need to check the length!)

Okay. I brought up the subject of control, so I'd best deal with it right now. If you're paddling whitewater—and that doesn't mean "running" a rapid, it means "playing" a rapid—I'm quick to concede that the control strokes you'll use are better done with a straight-shaft paddle. We'll talk about those strokes later. If, however, you're a "going somewhere" paddler, you can make a canoe do anything you need it to do with a bent-shaft paddle. And for probably ninety percent of your paddling, you can do it as well and more efficiently. If you couldn't, the folks who paddle marathon canoe races and the folks who race open canoes downriver in whitewater would be using straight-shaft paddles. They don't.

So much for the paddle—almost. If you're buying paddles, I suggest that a degree of equivalency be maintained between what the bow paddler gets and what the stern paddler gets. I've been in this game a long time, and all too often I've seen The Captain of the Ship buy himself the latest and lightest, and get the First Mate (otherwise known as "wife," because no girlfriend would put up with such nonsense) a heavy, clumsy club, which he wouldn't use as a spare, because "it's good enough." Get paddles that feel good and look good, and you'll use them more.

Your Life Jacket

Every state mandates that you have a U.S. Coast Guard–approved Personal Flotation Device, or PFD, on board for each passenger. When I'm teaching, I require every paddler in my class to wear a PFD, and I wear one myself. Learn to paddle while wearing a PFD and you won't feel uncomfortable with one on. Yeah, I know. Paddling's a barefoot sport, a sun-and-sand sport, and a PFD sort of spoils the image. So does drowning. Wear the PFD. Sure, there'll be times in non-threatening warm water on a warm day when you can slip out of the PFD. That's a judgment call. But you're just learning to paddle. You're just learning which situations are threatening and which are not. Until you know, wear the PFD all the time. If you're less than confident as a swimmer, wear the PFD all the time. It's a confidence-builder and a warm, cozy buddy when the chilly winds pick up.

What kind to get? The kind your canoe shop might call a "paddling vest." It looks like a vest made of closed-cell foam strips or soft foam covered with nylon, and it has a zipper closure and a waist belt that either ties or buckles. It should fit you comfortably; too tight is, well, too tight, and too loose means that it could ride up over your head when you least want it to. It shouldn't bite your neck, and it shouldn't bind under your arms. Your canoe shop can advise you on the fine points of it. Try it on and then paddle the air. If it chafes in the shop, it will chafe on the water. Get one that feels comfortable all around.

A good PFD will set you back $55 to $120. If that seems like a lot, consider that if it fits well, looks good, and is comfortable you'll wear it. And if you wear it, it will do you some good when you need it. You can get cheap orange horsecollar PFDs for about $15. You can get flotation cushions for about the same price. Either will fulfill your obligation under most boating laws. So why not get them? The horsecollar fits so badly that you won't wear it, and it's of dubious value as a protective device because it leaves your back unprotected. The flotation cushion is great for a lunch break, but do you really think you're going to be able to get to it if your boat overturns, or if you take a nose-dive out of your boat and the wind and current carry your boat and cushion away? Get a good PFD. Wear it. End of sermon.

Tricking Out Your Canoe

If you're not comfortable in a canoe, you won't paddle it much. And if you're not part of your canoe, you won't paddle it well—or easily. Fortunately, the tweaking you do for comfort is the same tweaking to fit you solidly in the canoe for good control and efficiency (Figure 1-3). The key is to have your seat, knees, and feet locked firmly in the canoe. Let's get to it!

First a little theory. When you plant the paddle in the water and pull, you're pulling yourself and the canoe to the paddle (and past it, because the canoe keeps moving after your stroke). If you're snug in your canoe, this works well. If you're not, then you slide around in the canoe. You lose power, efficiency, control, and if the truth be known, you aren't comfortable. Wasted effort and discomfort doesn't beckon you to go paddling again.

Comfort starts with the seat. Your canoe will have either some sort of bench-style seat (with a frame supporting a caned insert or nylon webbing) or a tractor-style bucket seat (which looks just like its name). The wonderful thing about a tractor-style seat is that it holds your backside firmly in place—giving you something to push against as well as preventing you from sliding around. You can add foam pieces to a bench seat to accomplish the same thing.

Either type of seat can be padded with thin, closed-cell foam of the sort backpackers carry. Some folks opt to enclose the foam in a comfy fabric. I suppose there's merit in that, but not in the damp maritime climate I live with on the shores of Lake Huron. If the seat pad were detachable, you could convince me. A seat pad held in place with Velcro might work fine. Remember, there will be hot, muggy days when you want air ventilating around your seat, so leave yourself the option to remove the pad. Also remember to provide a seat drain for the water on rainy days.

It's worthwhile having a seat that will hold your backside in place. That's so you can push against it. Your feet will be braced against some sort of solid object called, not surprisingly, a footbrace. For a bow paddler, the front flotation chamber is often used as a footbrace. For the stern paddler, a footbrace could be gear on the bottom of the boat, a dowel rod anchored to the stern seat by a cord, or a tele-scoping footbrace that can be adjusted for leg length. I like the telescoping footbrace better than the other alternatives. You may not always have gear when you paddle, and a dowel rod set-up isn't really solid, and the cord could tangle around your feet in a capsize.

Now don't forget your knees. Manufacturers design gunwales to be strong and attractive, but you want to lock your knees against the inside of that gunwale and sometimes it's a sharp edge. Ideally, your thighs should be parallel to the gunwale so you don't have to reach out to paddle over bent knees. Glue some foam along the inside gunwale of your canoe where your knees and thighs lock in for more comfort and better control.

We've been assuming you're sitting in your canoe and that's because we're talking about an efficient paddling technique with bent-shaft paddles. But the high priests of this game aren't so rigid as to disallow kneeling. If you're going to be a kneeler using a straight-shaft paddle, then you still need solid points of contact with your canoe. Start with a set of foam kneepads; they not only keep your knees soft, they keep your knees from sliding around inside the

Foam knee pad

"Tractor-style" seat

Adjustable footbrace

Traditional "bench" seat

Foam knee pad

Air chamber functions as bow "footbrace"

Figure 1-3: Outfitting your canoe—seats, footbraces, and kneepads

canoe. Glue the pads in place; they should be set comfortably apart in the chines of the canoe (where the bottom meets the sides). Whitewater paddlers install thigh straps to hold them in the boat better when kneeling, and I've known a flatwater paddler or two who uses them for the same reason.

If your seat is placed so low that you bump your armpits against the rails, raise the seat. If the seat is so high that you feel uncomfortable in the canoe, lower the seat. If the canoe doesn't ride level in the water with you and your partner in it, move the bow seat forward or aft to make the boat trim; move the stern, too, if you must. If you want to get really fancy—or just plain do the job right to begin with—mount a sliding seat in the bow. If that doesn't give you a level trim, mount a stern slider as well. If there's a substantial weight discrepancy between you and your partner, go directly to the bow and stern slider setup, or rig the canoe to allow you to mount an extra set of seats placed in such a way as to permit you to switch places.

Switch places? Isn't that heresy? Maybe for some, but if you paddle with this style you should be able to paddle bow and stern with anybody else who paddles this style. You'll be able to paddle from either side with aplomb. And if you're used to being the Captain sitting in the stern and barking orders to the Mate, you're in for a rude awakening. A pleasant awakening, actually. It's easy to flip a bass bug at a log when you're in the bow! (Don't let Molly read this, or I'll be back in the stern again!)

Anyway, set the boat up so you can trim it level without gear, so you can keep your butt fixed in place when you're working, and so you have somewhere to plant your feet. If you can do all that yourself, fine. If you can't, go to your friendly local canoe dealer and solicit his help. While you're there, you might ask him why in hell he didn't sell you a boat with a bow slider and footbraces in the first place!

Getting into Your Canoe

Oops! Forgot something. Would you believe that getting into and out of a canoe is when most upsets occur? It's true. And believe me— nothing can squelch the joy of a day on the water like a thorough soaking before you even get in the boat!

Canoes are stable craft. It's paddlers that make canoes unstable. Set a canoe adrift in whitewater or on a big lake when the whitecaps are rolling, and the canoe will take care of itself. Add two paddlers, and you raise the center of gravity and the roll center of the canoe, and the canoe loses some of its rock-solid stability. A modicum of common sense and a pinch of learning will compensate for that once you're on the water. But going from the bank to the water is tricky. A canoe isn't very stable when its bow is on shore, its stern balanced precariously on the river bottom, and nothing but air under its middle. It also isn't very strong. Canoes are designed to be strong when they're supported by water, not when they're balanced precariously on both ends. More canoes are tipped over—and more canoes are damaged—getting in and getting out than are damaged even on whitewater streams.

I don't want to talk this point to death. This isn't exactly a spiritual crisis we're dealing with, after all. There are many ways to enter and move around in a canoe, depending on circumstances, but all of them depend on two things. The first is to keep your weight-bearing foot on the centerline of the canoe. The second is to balance the canoe side-to-side by transferring some of your weight to your hands as each holds on to a gunwale of the boat.

Here's one way to get the job done. Put the entire boat in the water parallel to the shore in water a few inches deep. While you're learning, put your paddles in the canoe where (1) you can reach them easily, and (2) you won't trip over them. (Later on, after you've done this a few times, you'll keep hold of your paddle with one hand while you get in and out because a good canoeist always hangs on to his paddle!) Both paddlers grasp both gunwales (rails) of the canoe to keep it steady. You can face each other, or both face forward. One of you, often the stern partner, gets in first.

Now do like I already told you: keep your body bent over—to keep your center of gravity as low as possible—and step into the canoe, placing your foot right smack in the middle of the canoe right over the keel line. Balancing your weight on both hands and your foot, swing yourself in and kneel or sit down on the seat. One more time now: hands on both rails, body low, knees flexed, first foot goes dead in the center of the boat. Once you're in and settled, your partner will get in the same way. While he's doing that, you might want to lean the canoe a little bit to the side and put your paddle on the bottom like a pole to stabilize the canoe while he gets in.

When you're both seated comfortably, pick up your paddles. Your feet may be wet, but that's no big deal. The rest of you is dry, and the boat is floating freely, awaiting your further command.

Now that you know how to get in and out, place a foot in the center of the canoe and stand in a crouched-over position with your hands on the gunwales, sort of like a sprinter ready to come out of the blocks. Put some weight on your hands and rock the boat back and forth. Feel pretty comfortable? Can you wave your other foot in the air behind you without feeling nervous? Good; if you keep your weight centered, low, and balanced your canoe will take care of you—and that's a good thing to learn!

Now there are fancy sculling maneuvers that you can use to move the boat into water deep enough for paddling. And these maneuvers look sharp and make you feel good about yourself. Someday we'll talk about sculling, but it will be at another time and place. For now, gently push yourself away with the paddles. I promise I won't tell anybody that you did it that way if you won't tell anybody that I told you to do it.

Canoe Paddling

The Basic
Forward Stroke

2

Over ninety-five percent of your paddle strokes will be made to move your canoe in a straight line, and ninety-five percent of the rest of your strokes will be simple control and turning strokes that are little more than forward strokes taken in a different direction other than parallel to the keel line of your canoe. You don't have to be a rocket scientist to understand that learning a good forward stroke gives you a solid foundation for virtually all of your paddling.

Now before we make a mad dash to the water with canoe and life jackets, stick a piece of tape on the power face of your paddle. That's the side of the blade that is used for the forward stroke—to pull the canoe through the water. If you have a bent-shaft paddle, you're going to have to figure out which is which. Usually you can tell by the comfort of the grip; most bent-shaft paddles have a grip that feels comfortable one way and not the other. If you need another clue: when the shaft is vertical, the blade should angle forward. (The drawing will show you; see Figure 2-1.) If you have a straight-shaft paddle, pick a side for the tape; until you put the tape on, either side can be used as the power face. Done that? Great! Now let's get on the water and get to it.

In the last chapter we were on the water, floating free, with enough depth under the hull that you won't bash your paddle on the bottom. Now before we go anywhere, I have to tell you Robert's Rule #1: "Two shall not paddle on the same side of the canoe, lest the sea

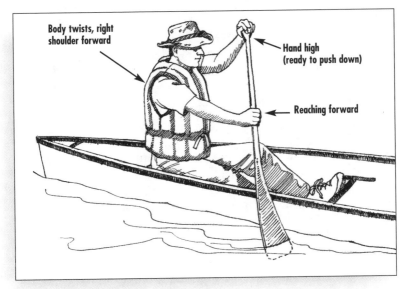

Body twists, right shoulder forward

Hand high (ready to push down)

Reaching forward

Figure 2-1: Paddling position, ready to go

rise up and bite them in the butt."
So you're going to have to agree
who paddles on which side. It
won't matter for long, because
using bent-shaft paddles, we're
going to switch sides (together)
anyway. If you're using straight-
shaft paddles, it makes a lot of
sense for the stern paddler to be
on his or her favorite side because
the stern paddler is primarily
responsible for the direction of the
canoe, and we want that job done
as well as it can be. So let the stern
paddler choose a side; the bow will
paddle the other side.

While we're at it, I may as well
tell you Robert's Rule #2 (see
Figure 2-2) : "Two shall paddle
together, in sync, harmoniously,

Figure 2-2: Paddling opposite sides in perfect sync

Canoe Paddling

simultaneously, lest the canoe rise up and dump them in the drink."
How do you do that? It's easy—the stern paddler watches the bow
paddler and exactly matches the stroke rate.

So let's sum up. *You and your paddling partner paddle on opposite
sides and paddle together.* That's not so hard to remember, is it?
Good—now you won't look like rookies on the water!

Making the Canoe Go

Okay, now hold the palm grip—that funny little knob on the top of
the paddle shaft—with one hand; that's your "upper" hand. With
your other hand (the "lower" hand), grasp the paddle shaft about
two to three hand-widths above the shaft from the top of the blade.
Avoid a death grip on your paddle, hold it with the same tenderness
as holding a baby; after all, we want to be relaxed and have fun at
this game.

Now, sit erect but "easy," like a big league shortstop waiting on the
pitcher to throw the ball. To begin the stroke (Figure 2-3), rotate your
upper torso a little, leading with the shoulder of your lower hand.
Place the pad-dle in the water, with the blade vertical, or nearly so,
your arms nearly straight and away from your body with your upper

Figure 2-3: Forward stroke

hand high and out over the water. Rotate your upper torso back to neutral, pulling on the paddle with your lower hand and pushing down the paddle shaft with your upper hand as you go. Lift the paddle out of the water and using the same rotation, put the paddle back into the water, again pulling yourself up to the paddle by "unwinding" your upper body ... and so on. It's a simple repetitive move that, in a sense, keeps the shoulder of your top hand almost still and the rest of your upper body rotating around it. The key here is a body twist (rotation) that brings major muscles of the back into play.

Okay? Erect but not stiff? Rotating your upper body around the fixed point of your "off-side" shoulder? Rotating back to neutral and lifting the paddle out of the water? Paddle blade vertical or nearly so? Good. Even if it doesn't feel normal, it's a good start. With time and practice it will feel natural.

Your arms really don't do much in a good touring stroke. It's not strictly correct to say that they do nothing, but the real engines that drive the boat are the large muscles of your back, shoulders, and belly. And they can drive the boat easily because your feet are planted and your backside isn't slipping, and you have a firm foundation against which to work.

Some practice exercises will help you get the feel of paddling correctly. For a few strokes, lock your elbows so your arms are straight and rigid. Now ... paddle! It feels awkward, but it makes the boat go, and do you feel your back doing the work? And do you notice how you have to rotate to make it work? Good ... that's the feeling you should have in your back all the time when you're pulling your canoe through the water.

Now focus on your upper hand. Pretend it's a piston that simply moves up and down. Your hand is going to go high, then push down the paddle shaft, then straight back up high to prepare for the next stroke. Make it go straight up and down. You'll find your stroke will be much more vertical, you'll feel the power of your downstroke shifting to the angled blade in the water, and you'll notice your lower hand sliding out to the side just enough to clear the blade above the water on the recovery part of your stroke.

When you can combine the piston action of the upper hand with body rotation so you're pulling with your back, you're on your way to developing an efficient, powerful forward stroke. You don't always have to paddle with dramatic action, but your paddling engine will be

Canoe Paddling

idling along and can be revved up as needed to handle wind, current, or a race.

Now here's the tricky bit. You've paddled a few strokes, and the boat is starting to move along. But it's turning to the side on which the bow paddler is paddling. And it may be bobbing and diving and feeling wiggly. Let the boat glide nearly to a stop and start over again. Bow paddler: Do that simple, repetitive stroke in a regular, metronome-like rhythm. It needn't be fast; that comes with practice. One stroke every two seconds is just fine for starters, remember you're learning a habit pattern, and you want to get it right. Stern paddler, keep your bow paddler's tempo. Put your paddle in the water at the same time, rotate your upper body through the same degree of arc, take your paddle out of the water at the same time, and so forth. Just like dancing together.

Going Straight

By now the old canoe should be running along pretty nicely, but it still wants to turn away from the side the stern paddler is on. That's simple physics. If you look at a canoe with two paddlers in it, the stern paddler's paddle is farther away from the centerline of the canoe, and his/her stroke is also nearer to the canoe's center of rotation than the bow paddler's stroke. The canoe *has* to turn away from the stern's stroke. (Sorry, stern buddy, but you're not "overpowering" your partner. Unflex those biceps, spit out your chew of Red Man, reduce the testosterone, and unclench!) The canoe will continue to turn unless you do something to stop it from turning.

Now back at good old Camp Yookintipovurtu, in the days of your youth, you learned something called a J-stroke from a camp counselor who was bored silly, preoccupied with dreams about somebody in a red swim suit at the camp across the lake, and who didn't know much about canoeing to begin with. And the old J-stroke worked, after a fashion. You had a gut feeling that it scrubbed off a lot of the canoe's speed, and was sort of like accelerating away from a stop light while stabbing the brakes at the same time, but it got you there. Well, your gut was right, and although there is a place for a J-stroke, we won't be using it right now. You'll be doing something else.

Think about this: If the bow paddler is paddling on the left and the stern paddler is paddling on the right, and the canoe wants to turn left after eight or ten strokes, what's the easiest way to stop it from turning? Right you are: Switch sides! In fact, that's what novices do when they first get in a canoe and realize that it's not going straight. But if you watch, there is no rhythm to their switches, and the canoe is usually out of control—wildly careening from one side to the other like a drunken sailor. Still, the switching-sides theory works; after all, that's how racers paddle long distances at hellishly high speeds. But unlike the novice, we're going to switch with rhythm and a pattern to keep our canoe under control.

When to Switch Sides

Most modern canoes are designed to hold a reasonably straight course with little effort because these canoes are used to going somewhere (touring), and a canoe that requires constant attention to make it go straight isn't a pleasant boat for touring. In technical terms, touring canoes are shaped to provide lateral resistance at their stems. It takes a nudge—and in some cases more than that—to overcome that lateral resistance. Once the canoe is up and running, it'll go maybe ten strokes before it begins to turn significantly. One of the more subtle tasks of paddling is to figure out when the canoe wants to start that inexorable turn to the bow paddler's side, and when to switch together—on command—before the canoe is off-course and out of control. While you're learning, try switching every six to eight strokes, and adjust as needed.

The stern paddler calls the switch, *not* because he is the boss but for two better reasons: The stern paddler can see better and more quickly that the canoe is slipping off course, and the stern paddler can see whether or not the bow paddler has heard the command and switched. The bow paddler doesn't have that option.

Timing counts for something here. Stern paddler: Call the switch at the start of a stroke. This gives the bow paddler a chance to get out of the autopilot mode and react to your call, switching sides at the completion of the stroke. Stern, keep your call a simple mono-syllable. "Hut!" is the almost universal call the racers use. It's short, audible, can be grunted, and in legendary racer and designer Gene Jensen's words, "You can say it when you're about ready to throw up." Yes, it does sound silly when you first start doing it. It may even sound intrusive in a paddling situation where quiet is called for, although you will learn to adjust the call to the situation. When it's quiet, a barely audible call works fine; when paddling in a wind, you may have to sing it out because your bow paddler may not be as able to hear your call. In any case the silly feeling passes quickly. You'll find after fifteen minutes that you can maintain a normal conversation and still say "Hut!" when you need. You (Hut!) won't even hear yourself saying it (Hut!) after a while, and even if your (Hut!) friends think it's nonsense (Hut!), I guarantee that (Hut!) you'll get to the takeout (Hut!) long before they do (Hut!) and have first dibs (Hut!) on the cold beer (Hut!) and cheese and French bread (Hut!) you stashed in the car.

Now some folks figure that if you're going to switch sides, you might as well do it automatically on a regular count, like every 6 strokes. Canoe designer David Yost calls it "The Idiot Six"—six power strokes and a switch. It works to maintain direction, but it's a short cut to mediocrity. For one thing, paddling is supposed to be fun (remember?) and counting "one—two—three—four—five—six—switch, one—two—three—four..." as you paddle isn't the kind of fun we're talking about here. Besides, there are times when you will need to switch in response to wind, for a change in direction, and for turns. More later; for now, become proficient in switching on command and the rest will work out better.

How to Switch Sides

At the completion of the forward stroke, start to remove the paddle from the water and recover as usual. But instead of lifting your top hand for the upward cycle of the "piston" stroke, release your top hand from the grip of the paddle. Meanwhile, your lower hand (on the shaft) is going to pass the paddle across your body to your "new" lower hand, the one you just released. It's not unlike a runner passing a baton in a relay race, except you're going to pass the paddle to yourself. It's best if the new lower hand grabs the paddle shaft under the passing hand. Make the exchange well out in front of your body. As your new lower hand takes control of the paddle shaft, slide your other hand up the shaft to find the grip as you place the paddle in the water for the first stroke on the other side.

You can practice this sitting on an armless chair. It takes a few minutes of feeling clumsy, but it's easy to learn. If you really want to feel silly, go outside with your partner and your paddles, stand (or sit) in bow/stern alignment, and paddle the air, with the stern calling

Lower hand passes off to "new" lowerhand

Figure 2-4: Switching sides

the switches. Sounds dumb. Looks dumb. Works like a charm! It gets you into a "team" mode very quickly. The bow must react to the stern's call, and the stern must respond to the bow's tempo. Dancin', baby! Dancin'!

Now that you know how to switch to maintain direction efficiently without scrubbing off speed with exaggerated correction strokes, you'll be pleased to know that maintaining speed and direction isn't the only reason for switching sides; it's just one of the reasons. The others? Switching sides (Figure 2-4) lets you equalize the work load on your joints, tendons, and muscles; it enables you to make the most powerful, most stable turning strokes; and it gives you a real edge in windy conditions.

A Quick Review of the Basic Forward Stroke

I prefer to think of the forward stroke as the "power stroke" because you use it to provide power in all directions. It's a little fussy to get right, so let's break it down again and add a few subtleties while we're at it.

Canoe Paddling

Sit erect but relaxed. You should be attached to your canoe with three body points: feet on a footbrace, knees "grabbing" the inside of the gunwale, and backside set solidly in the seat. Keep your legs out in front of you on the footbrace, but not stiff. Thighs should be parallel and against the gunwale; I don't want your bony knees sticking up in the air—they get in the way of a good efficient stroke! When it's time to "lock" yourself in the boat, flex your feet against the footrest and your knees will better grip the gunwale (you did install some foam, right?) and your butt will be pressed firmly in the seat. As you tighten yourself in the canoe, you will be able to control the canoe with your hips.

Hold the paddle loosely, with your arms extended but not stiff. Your forward stroke should be done comfortably out in front of you. If you are paddling close to your body, there is no room for power and efficiency, and your switching action will be difficult.

The power of your stroke comes from engaging the large muscle groups in your back and shoulders. As you progress, you'll become increasingly aware of starting the stroke from your instep, and you'll feel the power flow from the soles of your feet, through your legs, up your rotating torso and along your arms to the paddle. In fact, you'll begin to notice your legs flex with each pull, and your arms will become simply a "connector" to the paddle to transfer the power generated by your rotating torso. To put power into the paddle blade, rotate your upper body around the point of the shoulder of your upper hand. That's the pivot point, not your waist.

Your arms work together as one unit. You don't push with your upper hand and pull with your lower hand. Neither do you cock your lower arm for little extra snap on the stroke; the power comes from the back and shoulders. Think of settling the power into your *latissimus dorsi* muscles. Feel it? Your arms and hands rise and fall; the proper motion is almost up and down, like a piston, rather than forward and back.

As you get better at this game, you'll find that you tighten up your abdominal muscles a bit with each stroke, and when you really want to make time, you'll straighten up almost imperceptibly as you re-cover, relax your gut to let a little air sneak in, and tighten down hard in a very brief isometric as you apply power.

You'll notice words like *brief* and *a little* sneaking into this explanation. Here's why. If the tip of your paddle blade travels more than 5 to 7 inches at the point of maximum power, your forward stroke is too long. Remember that your maximum power is developed when the paddle blade is within fifteen degrees of either side of vertical. Anything more disturbs the progress of the boat. The bend in your paddle takes care of the forward fifteen degrees and your slight rotation and pushing down with your upper hand takes care of the back fifteen degrees. You don't need much rotation; it should be quick, and your paddle should be removed from the water as your shoulders come back to square.

Think of the whole operation in terms of turning a merry-go-round on a playground. Once you get the merry-go-round moving, all it takes is a quick little push on each bar to sustain the movement— quick, frequent, and easy. The idea is to not let the merry-go-round slow down at all before you give it another little push. It's the same with a canoe: Once moving, all it takes are quick pushes against the water to keep it moving—quick, frequent, and easy. That's what your paddling should feel like ... flick ... flick ... flick ... and the canoe moves smartly along.

Okay, okay. I hear you! You're not a racer! Neither am I any more. So just slow the stroke down a little to where it's more comfortable, and don't "uncoil" as hard, that's all. Keep the stroke light and easy, but continue to use your whole body. Don't paddle sloppily when you're not in a hurry. In fact, greasing through a backwater to sneak up on a raft of Canada geese is the time to learn to paddle with subtle power and elegance. (And it's the time to learn to say "Hut" *quietly*!)

There's hardly any movement with this stroke. You're still; you're centered over your butt. You're not lunging forward with each stroke to "get more power" because you can't get more power by lunging forward and "punching" your upper hand out. You get the power from your rotation and you drive against the paddle grip, but it's a downward drive, and happens only after the blade has been "set" in the water.

Some paddlers pull so hard that the bow of the canoe rises and falls. That's called *porpoising*. Usually the paddler is lunging and straining. That's no good—it wastes energy. You want to go forward, not up and down. Watch a good paddling team. Some unseen hand pushes their canoe along with no apparent effort. Maintain your good stroke technique and pay attention to your bow; it should move along smartly without even a hint of up-and-down motion.

Canoe Paddling   **19**

Is your paddle exchange smooth, even, and efficient? Go slowly at first so you won't rush the switch. Focus on fully completing the stroke before making the exchange; shortening up the stroke because you're in a hurry to switch costs you pulling power and efficiency. Similarly, you should work on getting a full, strong first stroke after an exchange. To practice, agree with your partner to switch on every stroke without command. Go slowly and make the switches and strokes in a metronomic cadence. As you become proficient, slowly increase your paddling cadence until you are able to make an exchange at speed without missing a beat.

Taking the Paddle out of the Water

To take the paddle out of the water—the techy term is *recover*—use the same motion as you did to put the paddle in the water, but in reverse. Up and down, not forward and back. As your upper hand lifts, you'll find your lower hand will have to swing out just enough so the paddle blade exits and clears the water on its way back to being planted again. This whole motion is called a *high recovery* and is most efficient for minimal motion and quickness. Occasionally when you're bucking the wind, taking your time, or trying to look elegantly stylish, use a *low recovery*. Let both hands drop toward your lap and wind your body back up as you swing a horizontal paddle across your lap. When you do, you'll have to raise your upper hand quickly at the end of the recovery in order to plant the paddle properly in the water for the next stroke.

Check Your Technique

While you're paddling, occasionally check your technique. Is your upper hand high and over the water with your paddle shaft vertical? Is your lower hand consistently above or at gunwale level as you paddle? Is your head still, not bobbing around from side to side or lunging forward? Is your paddle shaft vertical as you pull your forward stroke? And is the face of the paddle blade perpendicular to the direction you are pulling? Good! You've got it figured out. Feels good, doesn't it?

Correction Strokes

For all my talk about the basic forward stroke, it is only one of the tools in your canoeing tool kit. It's the fundamental tool, no doubt. But you can't build a cathedral with just one tool. So let's open the tool box, poke around inside, and see what we find.

When I'm teaching a class on the water, I hardly ever give a name to a stroke until the students have already absorbed most of what they need to learn about it. Why? If I just tell you and show you how to do something, you treat it as a straightforward learning experience and simply do it. But if I tell you, "Now we'll learn the draw stroke," you're apt to start thinking something like, "Oh-oh, this sounds tough," or "Oh, no, I've never been able to do this."

It's tough to disguise names in a book, though. Readers like to have landmarks, like chapter titles and headings, to help them find their way through the maze of less-than-deathless prose. Okay, so here goes: We're going to talk about the draw stroke. You have thirty seconds to be anxious.

There are two kinds of draw strokes, static and active. The difference is simple. The active draw stroke is basically our old friend, the power stroke. There's no way to mess this one up—you already know it! It's simply a power stroke done at an angle of up to ninety degrees to the keel line. There are a few subtleties but it's a straightforward moving stroke; you pull on the paddle. The static draw, which is called a *post* by marathon racers and a *Duffek* by whitewater paddlers, is a stationary stroke; you simply hold it in place. We're going to use the racers' term because it's shorter and cooler than "static draw."

The Post, or Static Draw

Let's first look at how the post (Figure 3-1) works. You're in the bow, paddling along at a modest pace. On a whim—and bow paddlers can indulge in whims—you stick your blade in the water just alongside your hip, blade parallel to the keel line of the canoe, and the power face of the paddle facing the canoe so that you can see the tape you put there. The blade should be as vertical as you can get it. If you're paddling with a straight-shaft paddle, it's easy to keep the blade vertical—just keep the shaft vertical. But if you have a fifteen-degree bent-shaft stick in your hands, then you're going to have to push that upper hand out over the water far enough to bring the blade to vertical. And that's okay; in fact, to make it work keep your lower hand right close to the canoe—there's nothing that says this stroke has to be done away from the canoe.

Okay, now what happens? Nothing? You're absolutely right— nothing is happening. The blade just slices through the water as cleanly and quietly as you could ask. Now here comes the stroke ... keep the paddle located exactly where it is but turn the blade by rotating your upper hand (and wrist) so as to turn the *leading edge* of the blade *away* from the canoe. A good angle is thirty to forty-five degrees from the keel line of the canoe. That piece of tape you put on the power face will now be "looking" at oncoming water as you "open up" the power face of the blade.

You will now feel a sideways pull from the paddle, and as the water pushes the paddle away from you, you're hanging on to the paddle so it takes you along with it, and because you are connected to your canoe, the paddle pulls the bow of the canoe to the side. Right? Put more angle on the paddle blade, and it pulls you even faster to the side. Put less angle on the blade and it moves you sideways more slowly. If you put too much angle on the blade, what happens? It slows the boat down as if you put a brake in the water. The post is used by the bow paddler to turn the bow of the canoe toward the paddling side.

Upper hand well outboard to get blade vertical in the water

Blade angle about 30°–40° to center line of canoe

Figure 3-1: Post, or static draw

Before we set the post aside for later use, try turning the angle of the blade the other way. Oops! Did you get wet? I'm sorry—I guess I forgot to mention that if you have the wrong angle on the blade it will try to dive under the boat, banging into the side of the canoe. If you're cruising at speed, it can actually catapult you into the drink. So practice putting the post into the water with the correct blade angle already set. Do it a few times: power stroke—post—power stroke—post. Pretty soon you'll have it so you don't even have to think about blade angle. And one last tip. When you're finished "posting," simply slice the blade forward in the water and begin a power forward stroke. Neat, huh?

Draw Stroke

Active draw sounds like something a busy bartender does when faced with orders for twelve pitchers of draft from a thirsty crowd of paddlers. We'll just use the term *draw* because we're already calling the static draw a "post." A draw pulls the canoe toward the side the paddler is paddling on. Either the bow or stern paddler can draw, and it's a powerful correction stroke.

The draw (Figure 3-2) is actually a power stroke. It's your basic forward stroke but done *perpendicular* to the keel line of the canoe, not parallel to it. Many of the same rules apply. Turn your upper body so you're facing the side on which you're paddling. Now, with your arms well away from your body and both hands out over the rail, do a forward stroke. That's right. It's just a forward stroke perpendicular to the keel line. Right down to all the body rotation you can muster! This will move your end of the canoe over to the paddle; it will "draw" the

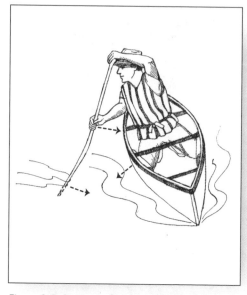

Figure 3-2: Draw stroke

canoe to the paddle, which is why it's called a "draw." Of course, by that reasoning, a forward stroke could be called a "draw" too, because it draws the canoe up to the paddle as well. But then . . . ah, forget it; this isn't a semantics course.

But there is one important difference. When you pull on a forward stroke, the paddle is in the water, the canoe is pulled to the paddle and simply moves past the paddle and all is well. When you pull on a draw stroke your paddle blade is in the water and the canoe is moving toward it. If you don't do something with the paddle blade, the canoe will run over it, and before you're able to let go of the paddle, you'll be pole-vaulted over the rail and into the water. Your partner will be much amused—unless you also dump the canoe!

There are two ways to avoid this difficulty. The easiest way is simply to slice the blade out toward your rear by dropping your upper hand forward. This works, but it's not elegant, and there's no point looking clumsy when you can look good. So instead of lifting the paddle from the water, keep it in the water and do an underwater recovery into another draw. Here's how. At the completion of the draw, point the thumb of your upper hand away from the boat as close to ninety degrees as you can manage, and push the paddle, with its blade feathered perpendicular to the keel line of the canoe, back out again with your lower arm and shoulder. Once in position, rotate your upper hand back to the power stroke position.

Notice that your upper hand hardly moves at all in a draw. It's well outboard of the rail and essentially stays there in one spot while you provide power, rotating the shoulder of your lower arm to pull the blade toward you.

Pry

Some paddle strokes are "antagonistic"—what one stroke will do, its antagonistic stroke will undo. The draw stroke has an antagonistic stroke. It's called a *pry* (Figure 3-3), and it moves a paddler's end of the canoe away from the paddling side. Start with your paddle alongside the gunwale with the blade parallel to the side of the canoe and the power face—the taped side—facing you. Using your lower hand as a fulcrum, raise your upper hand to slice the blade into the water until the paddle is vertical, keeping the paddle shaft against the side of the canoe. Now simply pull your upper hand toward you, levering the paddle off the side of the canoe. You've just used your paddle as a pry bar to move away from your paddling side, and that's why it's called a pry.

You can see that a pry is less effective with a bent-shaft paddle than with a straight-shaft because the bend of the blade tends to lift water rather than move the canoe sideways. And it is a stroke often used by straight-shaft paddlers of the whitewater type. Nevertheless, there are times when you will find it useful and it should be part of your tool kit. When you're

Fulcrum on side of canoe

Figure 3-3: The pry

doing a pry with a bent-shaft paddle, carry your upper hand far over the water as you slice the blade into place; that will tuck the blade farther under the canoe and give you a more effective pry.

Sweep Stroke

A sweep stroke looks just like you think it would. Instead of rotating your upper body and driving against a vertical paddle oriented parallel to the keel line, you sweep the paddle blade out in an arc, which moves your end of the canoe to the side while still maintaining way. Focus on maintaining a horizontal paddle as you sweep.

When doing a sweep stroke, don't stab at the water or try to thrash the water to a froth. Maintain the same sort of body rotation you use for your power stroke, with your hands away from your body, and maintain a rhythm. You usually can't sweep at the same tempo as you'd maintain for a power stroke because your paddle blade is in the water over a longer distance. But keep a rhythm and keep smooth. You've probably figured out that you can combine a power stroke and a sweep stroke to get a little of the benefit of each, and you're right. That's true with all your strokes. As you become more proficient as a paddler, you'll be blending them to accomplish exactly what you want. But while you're learning, practice doing the "pure" strokes.

If you're paddling solo, you can sweep from the bow to the stern—180 degrees of arc—and it will turn you quite nicely. But if you're paddling tandem and you're in the bow, sweep only in the quadrant from the bow to about ninety degrees to your side; if you're in the stern, sweep only from ninety degrees on the side to the stern of the canoe. If you sweep more than that, part of your stroke will actually be counterproductive.

Now that I've introduced the sweep, please remember that most paddle strokes can be done in reverse as well as forward. Try the sweep both forward and backward. (Don't turn your paddle around when you do a stroke backward; just use the other face of the blade.) Try it with the bow paddler sweeping forward and the stern paddler sweeping in reverse, and vice versa. Switch sides and play with the sweep. Get accustomed to powering the stroke with a body rotation rather than with your arms. Go for it! Pick a warm day in shallow water and see how much power you can put into the move. So you get wet! You wanted to take a swim anyway, didn't you?

The J-Stroke

Here's our old friend from Camp Yookintipovurtu, the J-stroke (Figure 3-4)! Hmmm. Must have found that at a flea market. But don't just toss it in the corner, my friend! Let's get some of the rust off the old J-stroke and put an edge on it, and we'll find it to be a most useful tool. We've been switching sides to keep the canoe running straight and true, but for those with straight-shaft paddles, the J-stroke is a key tool for tracking control. And it turns out to be helpful for the bent-shaft artists who want to keep those lean canoes on a little truer course.

Did you ever see one of those J-stroke diagrams in an old canoeing book? There's the J, lying flat, and the counselor told you to do it "just like the book says." So you pulled your butt up to the paddle, pushed out, and performed a short reversing stroke that raised hell with your elbow and just about stopped the canoe in its tracks. But it did keep you on course. Sort of. What you were doing, of course, was compensating for the tendency of the canoe to turn to your opposite side after each stroke. And that's what you'll be doing now, but we're going to make the rusty, old J-stroke a whole lot sharper, and you won't have to work as hard.

There was a time when I refused to use the term *J-stroke* because it was so widely misunderstood. I taught the J-stroke, but I called it a "hook stroke." But as I grew older and a little more respectful of tradition, I began calling it the J-stroke again. Besides, the American Canoe Association uses the term, and as an ACA instructor I'm obliged to use it.

Here's how to do it. Just before you complete

Figure 3-4: J-stroke

your power stroke, look at the thumb of your upper hand (on the grip). If your hand is relaxed, the thumb is either lightly touching the edge of the grip or, if you paddle with a very open hand as I frequently do, the thumb is pointing almost perpendicular to the keel line of the canoe. It's pointing abeam, if you will. What you need to do to create a small correction in the canoe's course—just enough almost to offset the slight turn created by the power stroke—is to give the paddle blade a little twist and flip outward just before the end of the stroke. Relax your upper hand. Let your thumb point abeam. And just before you finish your power stroke, twist your upper hand so that the thumb points forward. The twist doesn't have to be so exaggerated that your thumb ends up pointing right at the bow paddler, but it should be quick. And immediately after you point that thumb forward, get the paddle out of the water. Don't let it hang there scrubbing off speed. And don't try to help the process along by rotating your lower hand. Keep your lower hand loose and let the shaft rotate within your grip.

The most skillful J-stroke is the one that makes the smallest correction necessary to keep the boat tracking straight. That's the most efficient correction, and the one that best maintains the speed of your boat.

Backing Up

To backpaddle a canoe, rotate slightly toward the side on which you're paddling, so you start the reverse stroke about where you'd end the forward stroke if you over-rotated a bit. Lay the paddle blade horizontally on the surface of the water with both hands out over the water on top of the paddle. Now drive down with your lower hand and lift with your upper hand, rocking your body back so as to provide backing power with your back muscles. Keep the paddle shaft in the vertical plane (both hands over the water) throughout the backing stroke.

Take note that the bow paddler becomes the "stern paddler" when backpaddling a canoe. Because this person is facing the wrong way to see the overall direction of the canoe, it's difficult to learn to keep a backing canoe under control. But you'll find that by using draws, prys, and reverse sweeping strokes you will get the hang of it. Learn to do a "reverse J" to maintain a smooth backing course. As your back stroke (Figure 3-5) begins to exit the water, roll your upper hand back

Figure 3-5: Back stroke

and bring it across your body to shove the water to the side away from the canoe. Try it. Paddle backward occasionally just for kicks. Back out of the little duck hole you poked into. Keep at it, have fun with it, and you'll learn to play the game.

Will you do these strokes right the first time? No. It takes time. Practice and crank up the power as you feel more comfortable with your progress. And remember that practice produces perfection if you practice perfectly, and perfect practice produces pleasurable paddling. (I've always wanted to say that.)

Turning Your Canoe

4

As the editor of the largest paddling publication in the world, I get the opportunity to teach at a lot of canoe clinics. And it's always surprised me to find so many paddlers who are very concerned about how to turn their canoes, because that's actually the easiest part of boat management. The toughest thing to do with a canoe is to make it run straight and true in a wide range of conditions.

Let's look at what it takes to turn a canoe.

Turning by Not Correcting

The easiest way to make a gradual turn is simply to do nothing. You want to turn to the right? With the stern paddle on the left and the bow paddle on the right, if you don't switch sides or stick in a J-stroke, you'll turn to the right. With the bow paddle on the left and the stern paddle on the right, you'll turn to the left. We've just spent a lot of boat time learning how to keep a canoe from following its natural path, which is to turn. Just get out of the way and let it turn!

Want to turn a little faster? You can lean the canoe to the outside of turn, and you'll get a quicker response from your turning strategy. Why? Because leaning a canoe tends to raise the pointy ends out of the water and allows the canoe to "spin" on the rounded chine (the curved area where the bottom meets the side). This is easy to do;

since the stern paddler is already paddling on the outside of the turn, that person simply leans out a bit to put an outside lean on the canoe hull.

When you have the canoe leaned over a bit, your paddling stroke counteracts the risk of the canoe tipping too far—*as long as you are pulling on your paddle.* As you become more comfortable leaning, you'll find you can lean until the rail is nearly touching the water. Try it on a warm day in shallow water.

The stern paddler can aid a turn by using a sweep stroke instead of a pure forward stroke. (Remember: a stern sweep is done in the quadrant from about ninety degrees to the side all the way back to the stern of the canoe.) To adjust how quickly the canoe turns, use a combination forward/sweep stroke, using more of a sweep if you want to turn faster, more of a forward stroke if you want a lazy turn.

Turning by Paddling on the Same Side

Did I say that? Doesn't this violate Robert's Rule #1? Sure it does, but there are times when even Uncle Harry's rules can be broken, and this is one of them. Now be careful; when you paddle on the same side, you leave the "empty" side vulnerable because no one is at home to brace should the canoe tip in that direction. So you must compensate by keeping the canoe leaned toward the side being paddled. The stern paddler is going to have to get both paddles on the same side of the boat, either by calling "Hut!" and not changing when the bow paddler changes, or by switching sides without saying "Hut!" at all. Bow paddlers get really nervous when this happens without warning, so sing out "Same side!" before the event. That way, the bow paddler can brace his body in the canoe and anticipate the boat's action.

Lock yourselves in the boat by flexing your feet against the footbraces and holding your knees firmly against the foam pads on the side. Drop the outside hip. Both of you should lean the boat to the outside as you paddle. You'll find the canoe will carve a nice, smooth turn, although the canoe itself will wobble with each stroke because the torque produced by each paddler isn't canceled out by the two of you paddling opposite sides. If you *both* sweep, the boat will turn faster. (Bow paddler: Remember to sweep in your quadrant from the bow of the canoe to about ninety degrees to the side.) When the turn is complete, the stern paddler either calls "Hut!" or

Canoe Paddling

simply switches—whichever is needed to stop the turn and send the canoe back on a straight course again.

Turning with a Post

Turning by not correcting or by paddling on the same side is fine for big, sweeping bends and for course changes on a lake. However, they won't turn the canoe quickly. Let's talk about how to turn *fast*.

We're going to get into some real teamwork here. The stern paddler has to call the switch so the bow paddler is paddling on the side to which you want to turn. The bow paddler drops a post—a static draw—in the water while the stern paddler leans the canoe to the outside of the turn and paddles with a sweep. The bow paddler may feel as he's being pulled one way while leaning the other, and that's quite right. But as long as the blade stays in the water and is angled toward the direction of turn, the bow paddler's lean will actually be supported by the paddle as it pulls the bow of the canoe into the turn. (This support is called a *brace*—more about that later.) Remember to keep the blade of the post as vertical as possible, which means holding it close to the canoe if you're using a bent-shaft paddle. The angle of the blade will affect how fast the canoe turns, but if you have too much angle, the boat will slow down. You'll eventually develop a fine compromise between turning speed and boat speed as you gain more experience. For now, remember that if the bow paddle is making gurgling noises during the post, you probably have too much angle on the blade, or the blade isn't vertical in the water.

When you're working as a team, the bow can tell when a post is helpful, and simply does it when needed. If the stern needs some help with steering, as when you're fighting a wind, then a simple "Post!" command will ask the bow for assistance. Practice this turn until you can lean the rail of your canoe nearly to the water, and you'll learn that you can turn a long tripper more quickly than you ever imagined.

As the boat swings into the turn, it starts to turn slowly and then accelerates. Bow paddler: As you sense the swing of the boat to the completion of the turn, make your post into a forward stroke by slicing the underwater blade forward and then kicking in your power stroke. The boat will fairly blast out of the turn.

I know. You're not a racer. You're not interested in going fast. This isn't about going fast. It's about keeping the boat moving once you've got it moving. Any time you let the boat die in the water unintentionally, you have to crank it back up to a constant pace. It's like the difference in gas mileage between city driving and cruising down I–75, only we're talking about miles per gallon of sweat here.

Turning by Using the Active Draw

You already know that both the post and the active draw stroke move the bow of the boat toward the bow paddler's side. The active draw is a power move; use it when you need to pull the bow over in a hurry. If you don't need to move the bow over *right now*, don't waste your energy. Use a post instead. If you want to help your stern paddler turn, you can paddle with a combined active draw and a forward stroke, say at forty-five degrees, to maintain headway while pulling the bow of the canoe into a turn.

Turning for the Traditional Paddler

In the last chapter we looked at how the J-stroke will keep a canoe tracking straight. If you're using a straight-shaft paddle, the J-stroke becomes the primary tool for turning as well as for maintaining course. We've looked at how to turn a canoe by switching sides to take advantage of a canoe's natural propensity to turn when underway. But when paddling with a straight-shaft paddle in the traditional manner, switching sides isn't considered good form, so the J-stroke or some variation of it becomes the tool for turning as well as for maintaining course.

If you are using a straight-shaft paddle you can turn away from the stern paddler's side by not correcting at all, or you can use sweep strokes to accelerate the turn. But when you need to turn toward the side the stern paddler is paddling on, then a pronounced J-stroke is needed to do the job. This scrubs off a lot of forward speed, which is why marathon racers took to the sit-and-switch method using bent-shaft paddles. Whitewater paddlers, who need to make quick and powerful corrections using a straight-shaft paddle, use a horizontal pry off the stern to turn the canoe quickly toward the stern paddler's side. Carry the vertical power stroke well back, keeping it close to the side of the canoe. Twist the paddle by turning the thumb of the upper hand up, and pry off the side of the canoe with a quick push using the back face of the paddle—your paddle blade will be turned so the side with the piece of tape is facing you. Be sure the blade stays in the water so it has something to push against during the pry portion of the stroke.

Putting Your Tools into Practice

Now we've looked at how to make a canoe go straight and how to turn the boat with posts (static draws) and active draws from the bow. You can go straight—no mean accomplishment in these perilous times—and you can turn left and right using a variety of tools. Let's practice some of the elements of good turning strokes before we move on. And we will be moving on. There are a few more things you should have in your tool kit before you hit the wilderness.

One of the most pleasant ways to practice boat-handling skills is to paddle the perimeter of a lake, viewing every dock, every swimming float, every moored boat, every lily pad, and every overhanging branch as an obstacle to be avoided. I call this exercise the "lakeshore slalom." As you get better and better at this game, try to miss each object by as small a margin as you can (well, maybe not the moored boats). Start with the lily pads; they're a lot softer than rocks and docks while you learn and build your confidence. In a short time, you'll find yourself fairly screaming up to an obstruction and snapping the boat around it without scrubbing off hardly any speed at all.

If possible, practice your new boat-handling skills from both the bow and the stern. If you and your paddling partner can swap positions and still keep the canoe in level trim—it helps a lot if your respective weights aren't too different—swap paddling positions frequently. Paddle a lakeshore slalom; go have some fun. Remember, if you paddle this way you must be able to paddle bow and stern, and be comfortable working from both sides of the boat. Be patient. If you've paddled stern all your life, you'll probably be flummoxed by paddling bow, especially with a newcomer to the task of paddling stern. This is particularly true with husband-and-wife teams. Be supportive of each other's efforts, please. Be patient, please. You didn't learn to paddle your regular position in a day. Molly and I will switch positions in the boat regularly—sometimes three or four times in a single day of paddling. It keeps us fresh, it gives us a different perspective, it lets us use slightly different muscle groups, and it gives us the flexibility to jump in the right seat at the right time to serve the boat better. It also enables us to paddle with anybody who paddles this style. Any time, any river, any paddler.

As I've mentioned, this style of paddling requires the bow paddler to paddle on the side to which the canoe is to be turned, and the stern paddler to paddle on the opposite side. There's a good reason for this. An onside turning stroke is more powerful, more easily controlled, more easily turned into a forward stroke, and more stable than cross-body stroke. It also keeps the stern paddler in the right position for a bracing move or for other moves intended to deal with obstacles.

After you've learned your turning strokes and feel pretty comfortable with them, you'll sooner or later find yourself paddling in the company of a really experienced paddling team. You'll be amazed at how easily they slide their long, fast, touring canoe around obstructions. You're doing fine, not to worry. But you know their boat is harder to turn than yours. It's longer and leaner and it doesn't have as much rocker, and they're aggressive with that boat. They just flat-out scream into turns—and make the whole thing look so easy. How can you do that?

They're initiating their turns with a set-up stroke that makes their turning strokes that much more efficient. Let's set up for a right turn. You know the drill: bow paddler on the right, stern paddler on the left. You stick in a post or a draw—and you turn. They stick in a post or a draw, and the boat fairly snaps around. They could have done several things to initiate the turn and make it more effective. The obvious stroke is a stern sweep done before the bow paddler puts in the draw. More likely, the stern sweeps and the last forward stroke the bow paddler puts in before planting the draw is a forward stroke done maybe thirty degrees off the line parallel to the keel. It's generally called a *quarter draw*, although it can be done at any angle short of ninety degrees to the keel line. This quartering power stroke (or draw stroke—it does a bit of both) sets up the turn while still maintaining momentum into the turn. What does this translate to in terms of energy saving? A good bit, if you're turning a lot—like on a twisty river. It means that you go into the turn faster, carry your speed

Canoe Paddling   **35**

through the turn, and come out faster, and you've taken four or five fewer strokes in the process. This adds up to a lot more miles per gallon of sweat over the course of a day.

When you've gotten comfortable with these little tricky bits that save energy and get you across a lake or down a river looking like a pro, we'll show you how to take advantage of moving water in such a way that only the very best paddlers will be able to spot the exact strokes you used to turn your canoe. But that's for later.

For now, go take a run at that dock on the lake, initiate your turn a stroke or two before, and carve a turn around the end of it that will have the folks on the front porch of their cottage standing up and cheering!

A touch of the bill of your cap and a short salute is the proper acknowledgment. To ignore applause shows no class.

Maneuvering Your Canoe

H uh? C'mon, Uncle Harry! You've been telling me how hard it is to learn to paddle forward, and now you want me to paddle sideways and in circles? Are you sure that's just Gevalia Traditional Roast in your coffee cup?

Believe it. It's just coffee. And you need to know some maneuvers to take care of yourself in moving water. Sideslips and spins are necessary for boat handling in moving water. In still water, these skills probably won't be needed to save your boat, but they can save a lot of effort, and they'll have you lookin' good when you need to maneuver your canoe.

Spinning Your Canoe

Remember a few words back when we talked about draws and prys? Have you thought about what happens if both paddlers draw at the same time, or if both paddlers pry at the same time? Well, it's time to find out.

You've followed the bow of your canoe up a small but narrow waterway and when you get to the end you have to back out or turn your canoe around. Canoeists are the sort of folk who prefer to see where they are headed, so how are you going to turn around? What if you both reach out to your respective paddling sides and do an active draw stroke? Each paddler is pulling an end of the canoe toward his or her paddling side, and because you're on opposite sides, the boat will spin around the center yoke. You're on your way home. Almost too simple, isn't it?

As usual there are a couple points to consider. If you pull ninety degrees to the keel line, the canoe will spin. But if you want to spin a little more efficiently, the bow paddler should reach back a little more than ninety degrees, and the stern paddler should reach a little forward of ninety degrees. Now you're both pulling exactly in the direction that you travel on the circle defined by the spin. Try it; play with it. And while you're at it, check to see if your canoe is spinning around a single point, or if instead it goes forward or back a little while you're spinning. Practice until you can "spin on a dime."

Want to spin the other way? No problem. You can switch sides and use draw strokes, or you can each pry your end of the canoe away from your paddling side. You can also use pushaway strokes— more about that later. The pry approach isn't used so much by bent-shaft paddlers since this paddling style switches sides for control. Besides, a bent-shaft paddle doesn't pry very well because the angled blade tends to lift up water rather than push the canoe to the side. But if you're using straight-shaft paddles, spinning with paired pry strokes is quite powerful, even though not as quick as using draw strokes.

Know how to get better at paddling in sync? Spin! If you're in perfect unison placing your paddle in the water, pulling, and exiting the water, your canoe will spin silky smooth. If you're just a little bit off, it will wobble like a car with a flat tire. When you both can reach out and spin with draw strokes, leaving a (plastic) cup of water on your yoke without spilling, you've got it.

Sideslipping Your Canoe

Here's the situation. You're paddling the classic Adirondack Canoe route from Old Forge to the Saranacs (or to Tupper Lake, which is how I always preferred to end it). You've carried from Raquette Lake (it was windy, wasn't it?) into Forked Lake, and you've ridden a crisp westerly down the lake to the shallow, rocky outlet so you can register for a campsite with the ranger. You're zipping along at a good clip, and there's a large granite boulder a few boat lengths dead ahead, and four inches under the water. The water's gin-clear, but the waves were busy enough that you didn't notice it. What do you do?

You can backpaddle, and you'll probably stop in time to avoid the ego-deadening *thunk* that says, "You blew it!" to the whole universe. But with a loaded canoe, a good head of steam, and riding a following wind, you might not stop in time. You could turn, but the wind and waves might slow the turn enough for the stern to slide into or onto the rock. Help!

Help is on its way. Bow paddler: Stick in a draw—a hard draw. Stern paddler, your partner has just put in a hard draw, and you don't know why. *Trust your bow paddler.* Your bow paddler wouldn't do that out of a clear blue sky; there must be something up there that imperils the canoe. Don't think, don't ask, don't analyze. Push the stern of the canoe away from your paddle so that the canoe is moving forward and sideways—bow and stern aligned. If your bow paddler puts in another draw, just keep pushing the stern away from the paddle, and keep doing it until the bow paddler drops back into a forward traveling stroke.

Whew! That was close! You missed the boulder—and the canoe's still zipping along with very little loss of speed. Now's the time to backpaddle. It gets quite rocky here, and you'll have to pick your way through to the takeout at the ranger station.

You just *sideslipped* your canoe. It's exactly what the name says—you slipped the boat sideways to avoid an obstacle.

Now let's look at what you just did as a team. The bow paddler moved the boat sideways with an active draw stroke. If there had been a boat length more warning, the bow may simply have chosen a post, or static draw. The stern did the reverse of an active draw, a stroke called a *pushaway*. It's not an easy stroke to learn. It goes against all your common sense to move strongly away from the boat. Until you have the pushaway down solidly, remember that a reverse sweep will also push the canoe away from the paddle. The drawback to the reverse sweep is that it slows the canoe down more than the pushaway. If you come from a whitewater tradition or a classic tradition, you could use a pry stroke. I prefer the pushaway for touring paddlers using bent-shaft paddles.

Why the pushaway? A couple of reasons. It's smoother than the pry—and there are times when smooth is important. It leaves you in a position to move directly into another stroke, be it another pushaway, a brace, or a forward stroke. And because the power phase of the pushaway is about the same length as the power phase of the draw, the boat doesn't wiggle and jiggle. It feels stable at a point where you may very well need that feeling of stability. Let's look at the mechanics of a pushaway.

Pushaway Stroke

If you think of the pushaway as a reverse power stroke done ninety degrees to the keel line of the canoe, you won't go wrong. You know how to do a draw in the stern. Instead of starting the blade well away from the canoe as in a draw, start the pushaway with your torso nearly parallel to the keel line, and the paddle close to the boat. Slice the blade from behind until fully submerged with the power face (side with the tape) facing you. Apply power by rotating your upper body, directing the thrust away from the canoe with your lower arm and back. If you start with the paddle blade vertical, then your upper hand will be out over the water to begin. As you rotate the shoulder of your lower hand outward, remember that you're pivoting around the point of your upper hand's shoulder. Your upper hand hardly moves at all. The entire stroke is no longer than a draw; you don't have to end with your body hanging out over the rail.

To recover, you can slice the paddle out of the water or you can feather the paddle blade just like you did with the draw, except now you're returning the blade to the boat feathered. Do the stroke again if you need to. One pushaway in the stern for each draw in the bow is the rule of thumb, and please try to do the strokes together. Stern paddler, watch your bow paddler! Trust your bow. Follow your bow.

An Aside

Guys, if you're paddling with your wife or that special friend in the bow, here's the instance that shows whether you're a real paddler or Captain Macho. If you miss the rock, you both did your job. If you hit the rock, you both blew it! There is room in a canoe for a lot of things. Pierre Berton once observed that a Canadian is somebody who can make love in a canoe, and the irrepressible Philip Chester capped Mr. Berton's observation by noting that one had to know how to remove the center thwart. Room enough, indeed! But there is never room enough in a canoe for placing blame. There's room for figuring out what went wrong, and there's room for learning, but there's never room in a canoe for placing blame. Not in our canoe, and not in your canoe if you want to paddle with us.

Keeping the
Water Out

When you get right down to it, Steve Scarborough is right. There aren't many things you have to do with a canoe. You have to make it go forward and backward, turn it right and left, move it sideways, and keep the river in its proper place, which is outside and beneath the canoe. In a fair and just world, if you can make the canoe go forward and back, turn right and left, and move sideways, you've accomplished ninety-eight percent of what you have to do to keep the river in its place. Let me bore you with a story.

Back when Molly and I ran two outdoor shops and a cross-country ski area, we taught paddling a lot, both kayaking and canoeing. In winter the introductory kayaking classes were conducted in a swimming pool because in upstate New York water is frequently stiff in January and February. It took what could euphemistically be called "force of character" to keep the novice kayakers on track. They'd all come from a canoeing background and were incensed by the idea that we wanted them to learn to control their boats before we started teaching them to roll up. They finally got the idea that good paddling skills and sound mechanics would enable them to control their boats in such a way that they might not have to roll up as often. Bingo!

I'll show you two strokes that will keep the river in its place. Just remember that the better you manage all the other strokes, the less likely it is that you'll need these.

The Low Brace

The basic "Ohmigod!" stroke for canoeists and kayakers alike is the "low brace" (Figure 6-1). The common image of the stroke is one of a paddler falling on his paddle with a resounding slap that sounds like a beaver on steroids. The proper image to fix in your mind is a quick, subtle move that's mostly done by body position, and that flows directly into a stroke.

It's easier to learn a low brace in a solo canoe, or in a tandem canoe paddled solo from amidships. This doesn't mean that you can't learn it in a tandem canoe; you just have to maintain very good rapport with your partner.

Here's how it works. Hold the paddle as if you were taking a forward stroke, then place it horizontally, the knuckles of your lower hand down, the back (no tape) face of the blade flat to the water, away from the canoe and out beside your hips. Your upper hand should be about at your navel, your body comfortably erect and

Fulcrum hand

Figure 6-1: Low brace

elbows bent slightly. Now lean on the paddle and push down into the water. Start with a slight lean, and increase it as you feel comfortable. Recover by lifting your upper hand. Why? Because if you push down against the water with your lower hand, your weight will be too far outboard for the small paddle blade to support you. The blade will sink, with you attached to it.

When you lift your upper hand, your body moves against the roll of the boat and rights it. The paddle does very little beyond giving you a moment's purchase against which to move your body. Whether sitting or kneeling, to aid body movement, focus on driving your outboard knee up, while lowering the other hip. Once you have the mechanics of which hand to move under control, do it some more, but this time drop your head and shoulders to lower your roll center. Works better, eh? No surprise. You shortened the lever arm that wants to roll you over.

Let's get braver. Let your upper hand move farther and farther outboard as you practice, until both hands are outboard of the canoe's rails. Try to get the knuckles of your upper hand wet, and then the wrist. Drop your head and shoulders down inside the rails. Great! Your canoe was tipped far enough over to take in water, and you braced back up smoothly!

But sooner or later, you didn't make it. You needed one more brace, but the paddle sank out of sight before you could do it—and took you with it. For a simple low brace, with your upper hand inboard at about your navel, recovering the paddle is easy. For those times when the going is tough, you must get the paddle back to the surface so you can either brace again or move directly into an active stroke. As you lift your upper hand, turn it so your thumb points upward about thirty degrees, and rotate your upper body slightly toward the bow. This will drive the paddle in what looks and feels like a very short, powerful reverse sweep with the power directed downward. The blade will climb to the surface, and you're ready to brace again or move the canoe forward or sideways. Some paddlers call this move a "sweeping low brace."

This is fine—so far. Either paddler can and must be able to brace from either side of the boat and from either bow or stern. It's obvious that the stern paddler is in a position to execute a more powerful brace than the bow, but the boat doesn't always roll to the stern paddler's side! What do you do if you're the offside paddler? The simplest thing you can do is to drop your head and shoulders to lower the roll center of the boat, and then brace on your side. This gets your weight low and over the offside rail, and gets your paddle ready to catch the boat when it rolls back up.

If you're really hard-core about learning to brace, pick a warm day on a warm lake with a sandy bottom. Have a friend stand waist-deep in the water at the stern of your canoe and provide some unpredictable wave action for you. You need a solid brace most of all when you're not expecting it!

The High Brace

This is a classic maneuver. It's pretty, graceful, effective, and can be easily turned into a draw or a forward stroke. Most paddlers think of it as a bow stroke, but it works in the bow or the stern.

The high brace (Figure 6-2) looks almost like our old friend, the static draw, and if you take a paddling course from an American Canoe Association–certified instructor, the "high brace" will probably be referred to as a static draw, or perhaps as a Duffek. But the high brace is a little different. Draws, whether static or active, are done with your upper torso rotated so you can face your work. You don't

Pulls canoe back upright

Figure 6-2: High brace

always have the time to do that when you need a brace. The paddle shaft is vertical or nearly so when you draw because a draw is really a power stroke put in ninety degrees to the keel line of the canoe. But a high brace is usually done with the shaft angle more like forty-five degrees to the water, and the power of the stroke is directed both downward and toward the boat rather than toward the boat alone.

The dynamic part of the brace, the part in which you're exerting force on the paddle blade, is very short. The high brace is a favorite of sea kayakers and whitewater kayakers because it's really a part of their Eskimo roll. (You could make a strong case that the roll is nothing more than a high brace done from a very awkward position.) At any rate, you can tip a kayak to ninety degrees and the water won't come in. You can't do that with a canoe. The best application of the high brace in an open boat is to impart a short-term, steadying factor as you look for the right time to power out, turn, or sideslip. It's a particularly comfortable stroke for bow paddlers because they must always be prepared to apply power or set up a turn, and it's always easier to do those things from the firm platform of a high brace.

You may have noticed that a high brace doesn't always have to be a "high" stroke and the low brace isn't always done "low." What really differentiates them is the paddle face that applies the power to the stroke. The high brace is a power-face stroke, whereas a low brace is a pushing stroke using the back face of the paddle.

Practice, Practice, Practice!

Go from a draw to a forward power stroke to a low brace. Vary the sequence and blend your strokes. You should, in time, be able to go from any stroke to any other stroke—which well may include switching sides—with absolute ease, and without thinking about it. Paddling a canoe is blending the various strokes in your tool kit to take care of the boat. Remember: The only stroke you'll ever take that isn't part of a sequence is the last one you take when you come to shore.

Canoeing in Wind and Waves

I t always struck me as strange that all canoeing books spend countless pages telling you how to paddle moving water and whitewater, yet ignore how to paddle in wind and waves. The skills are related in the sense that good stroke mechanics, a calm demeanor, bone-deep teamwork, and a boat suited to the environment are essential. What makes paddling in wind and waves different? Several things.

To begin with—and maybe even to end with—there aren't any eddies on a big, windswept bay. You can't pop behind a rock in the current and find a little patch of calm in which to take a deep breath and make a plan for approaching what lies downstream. If you blow it, there's a long, long swim in store. It may not be as violent a swim as a heavy rapid can give you, but rapids end in pools, sooner or later. Lakes end at the shoreline—and a half-mile swim in the cold water of Lake Superior into the teeth of a wind is serious business. Finally, wind waves move, while river waves are generally stationary. Lake water pretty much stays in one place; lake waves move. Rivers water moves; river waves stand still.

There's one rule governing all big-water paddling. Write it indelibly on the back of your hand; chisel it into your memory. *If it's bad now, it will probably get worse.* Stay on shore or get to shore and wait it out. Yes, there are exceptions to this. You'll learn those exceptions as you grow in skill, experience, and wisdom. I grew up on a big lake. I live a half-mile by river from a very big lake, Lake Huron. I've spent a lot of time paddling in the Gulf of Mexico and other large bodies of water. And my partner, Molly, is as good a wind and wave paddler as you'll find anywhere. And we always have a couple of books and the binoculars and a bird guide with us for those days when we say, "No way!" Maybe we could have paddled. If we were in an emergency situation, like one of the party having had a heart attack, we would have paddled and made it. But we paddle for pleasure. And while it's fun to push the envelope sometimes—if the water's warm and the boat's empty—four hours of living on the edge in a survival situation isn't what most folks are seeking.

Paddling Upwind

Most paddlers get worried at the thought of running upwind, bucking the waves. But there's a big advantage to going upwind: You can see the waves coming and you can paddle *actively* rather than *reactively*.

If the waves aren't high, the simplest strategy is to run right up the gut and deal with them head-on. This puts a lot of spray in your bow paddler's face, and the boat loses speed because it's pitching up and down as much as it's going forward, but it has the charm of simplicity and it feels most predictably stable. The artist's way is to take the waves at an angle when they're high and run up into them at each momentary lull. Waves are never uniform. They'll come in sets of big ones and smaller ones, and sometimes you can find a relatively "flat" section that you can just hammer through.

When running straight upwind, switch sides frequently to flush the fatigue products from your muscles. You're working hard when you paddle upwind; do what you can to ease the fatigue. Learn to adjust the stroke cadence to match the cycle of the waves in order to smooth out the bouncing action of the canoe as much as possible. As you grow more skilled, and start attacking waves at angles when the opportunity presents itself, keep the stern on the downwind side of the canoe and the bow upwind. This puts the bow in position to draw up into the wind and waves as needed, and causes the stern paddler's forward stroke to drive the bow of the boat into the wind to keep from turning sideways and wallowing, or *broaching*, in the trough of the wave.

Quartering up into waves is a little more wiggly than running them head-on. The orbital motion of water particles in the crest of a wave is moving against the canoe at the time when the bow is most fully buried, and the canoe tends to be moved off a level orientation by the slope of the wave face. You've added another component of motion—roll—to the pitch component you deal with when running straight upwind.

If the waves are big and your course is upwind, a quartering strategy can help keep the water out of the canoe. The stern paddler should be paddling on the lee side of the canoe and should have a dependable bracing stroke. As the bow heads up the oncoming wave face, lean away from the oncoming wave, even though the wave crest wants to overturn the canoe the same way you're leaning. The stern paddler hits a forward/sweeping stroke as the wave hits, both to keep the bow from being knocked off course and to brace from over-turning. The lean away from the oncoming wave produces a greater hull surface to absorb the wave, keeping water out of the canoe. Just be sure that the bracing stroke is on time and solid, or you will help the wave overturn the canoe.

Paddling Downwind

Looks like fun, eh? You've just left the dock at Clearwater Lodge in Minnesota's Boundary Waters Canoe Area, fueled with anticipation and Clearwater's pancakes. You dawdled over coffee (you always dawdle over coffee at Clearwater Lodge), and the prevailing westerlies are already dappling the big lake with cats-paws, even at the lee shore. Wow! This is going to be an easy ride down to the 214-rod portage into West Pike!

Maybe not. Paddling a following sea with comfort and aplomb is one of the high points of the art. What should be a piece of cake can be turned into a horror show. A canoe running down the face of a wave gains speed rapidly, propelled by wind, wave, and the orbital flow of the wave itself. And when the canoe hits the trough of the wave, the bow buries, the canoe starts to run uphill, the orbital motion of the wave restrains its passage, and the stern "half" of the canoe is still accelerating. You're about to become a submarine—unless you're paddling a little off the wind. Then, the stern will swing crosswise as it slides down the face of the wave. Oh, my, Maynard, you told me this would be easy! What are we going to do?

Canoe Paddling   **49**

First, relax. If you're stiff, your head and shoulders are so much dead weight at the end of a three-foot lever arm that does nothing but raise the roll center of the canoe at a time when you least want a high roll center. Let the canoe roll under you as you paddle, using your hips and footbraces to keep control while your upper body rolls loosely and stays centered over your hips. (Now aren't you really glad you installed those foam knee pads in the canoe!) You can roll a canoe right up to the rail with no consequence if your nose is over your hips and relaxed. Stiffen up, and you're swimming for sure! Enjoy the sleigh ride. Revel in it, and in your control of the situation. Paddle with the calm of a Zen archer shooting out the flame of a candle. Feel the waves act on the canoe. Roll with them.

Strategies? In a following sea, bow maintains way, the stern maintains direction. Switches are always called by the stern paddler—and don't expect many. Stern generally paddles on the lee side of quartering waves, because a pushaway or reverse sweep will keep the canoe from sliding down the face of the wave and broaching in the trough. This also puts the stern on the side most likely needing a brace. Keep the canoe from accelerating (surging) down the face of a wave, keep it from stalling in the trough of a wave, and keep it from spinning on top of a wave as the wave bears under its middle—and you'll do just fine. Get in tune with the corkscrew action of quartering waves so you can anticipate the motion and enjoy the ride. Don't just drift through following seas, though. If you're moving at wave speed, you're at the mercy of the waves. Be more aggressive as your skills improve. Too much enthusiasm can sometimes get you into trouble, but too little enthusiasm will *always* get you into trouble.

Paddling in Beam Seas

Paddling across the waves requires the greatest degree of "feel" of all big-water paddling modes because there's more happening to the canoe in a beam sea.

Objects in the water tend to make the same motion as the water they displace. An empty canoe in a beam sea will follow the same circular motion as the orbiting particles in the wave that moves beneath it. There's not much relative motion between the canoe and the water. It's not rock-solid, but it's perfectly safe. But add paddlers to the canoe and the roll center is well above the waterline. This isn't a problem if you stay relaxed and fluid as the wave slips underneath. If you can't, the slight changes in lean that the canoe assumes—leaning leeward on the wave face, leaning windward on the back of the wave, and passing through a neutral point at the crest and the trough—will be magnified. Remember that the canoe will easily change from a leeward lean to a windward lean before the relatively high and heavy mass of your body will. Roll with the wave, using your hips to absorb the motion of the canoe as the wave passes underneath.

Those inexorable physical laws play a big part here. It doesn't take a huge sea to wreak havoc. One of the worst sea conditions to take abeam is one in which crests are separated by a distance equal to twice the waterline width of the canoe. Why? Because the wave period is so short that the canoe quickly passes through the leeward, windward, and neutral zones and the rate of roll is difficult to adjust to. And that's not a spectacular sea! For an average 17- or 18-foot canoe with a waterline width of 34 inches, this situation will occur at a wave height of about 10 inches in deep water, because a 10-inch wave in this situation will have a period (length from crest to crest) of about 68 inches.

The other "worst wave" to take abeam is a breaking wave (Figure 7-1), partly because the breaking wave violates the predictable orbital motion. The canoe starts to rise on the wave face and leans to leeward, and then gets hammered by water falling from the crest of the breaking wave. It doesn't take a lot of imagination to figure out what happens next! You've got a problem: you can either lean away from the break-ing crest and the wave will overturn you, or you can lean toward the crest to remain stable, but take the breaking water into the canoe. If you're really good, and a little bit lucky, you can split the middle and avoid both problems!

How to paddle in a beam sea? Stay loose. I know; you've heard that before. I meant it then and I mean it now. Enjoy, enjoy, enjoy. Keep the stern paddler on the leeward side, the bow on the windward. This keeps the effective brace where it needs to be, and also positions the bow paddler for the option to draw up, into, and over the wave crest and run for a set of smaller waves.

In big waves, it's sometimes useful to lean the canoe a bit to the lee side. This is a bit like weighting the downhill ski; your senses

Figure 7-1: Breaking wave

rebel against the notion. But it's a way to keep big waves and
breaking waves from dropping into the canoe. Stay alert. Nasty, steep,
short-period waves can be run by quartering into them as you head
for the bigger but longer-period stuff to run in the trough. It may
seem more intimidating, but it's a smoother ride.

It's worthwhile remembering that different hull shapes react
differently to beam seas (Figure 7-2). A canoe with a flat bottom

Figure 7-2: Different hull shapes in beam seas

BASIC ESSENTIALS

reacts more quickly and follows the contour of the wave, which can put it in a very unstable condition. A rounder hull has less freeboard, but reacts more slowly and will ride out a wave in a more upright attitude.

Some Common-Sense Advice

Dave Getchell, Sr., a wonderfully sensible man, once offered us some wonderfully sensible advice. If the wind is kicking up to the point at which paddling is a problem, and there's a shoreline that permits it, tow the canoe along the shore! It never occurred to me, so help me! I've since had occasion to use that advice—it works. Also, if you have to round a narrow point and the waves off the point look like killers, head for shore and see if you can portage across the point and put in on sheltered water.

Canoeing in Moving Water

8

This isn't a book about whitewater; neither is it a book about river reading. It's a book about paddling technique. But you won't be paddling very long before you encounter moving water. There are some things you should know about stroke combinations and how to handle a canoe in moving water so you can pass through safely and with confidence.

Ferrying

A *ferry* is using the current to slide a canoe sideways across a river. You can ferry across moving water with the canoe paddled upstream (*upstream ferry*; see Figure 8-1) or downstream (*backferry*). The backferry is the more difficult to learn because most canoeists are not adept at paddling backward; besides, it's difficult for a bow paddler to control direction of a canoe when they are facing forward and can't see the canoe behind them.

Let's look at the elements of a ferry and apply them to an upstream ferry. You're paddling upstream, preferably about as fast as the current wants to move you downstream. To move across the river (Figure 8-2), simply put a ten- to twenty-degree angle between your boat and the direction of the current, with the bow pointing in the direction you wish to ferry. Notice I said that the angle of the ferry is *relative to the current.* Some paddlers assume that a river's current runs straight between the parallel banks. It doesn't. Current direction

BASIC ESSENTIALS

in rivers is ever changing, and you'll have to adjust the angle of your boat to match changes in current direction. While the river current carries you across, throw in a little downstream lean to keep the big bad current from piling up on the upstream side of your canoe hull, and you're good to go.

Speed, angle, and lean are the components common to every ferry maneuver. The bow paddler's responsibility is to maintain speed; the stern paddler is responsible for maintaining correct angle with the current—primarily by using draws and prys, although sweeps may work as well. When you're first learning, it's probably easier if the bow paddler paddles on the upstream side of the ferry while the stern paddler paddles on the downstream side. Because the lean is provided by whomever is paddling on the side to be leaned, this allows the stern paddler to put the lean on the boat, and makes for easier correction strokes to maintain the proper ferry angle with the current.

There's really no difference between an upstream ferry and a

Figure 8-1: Upstream ferry

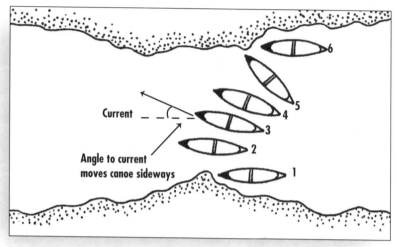

Figure 8-2: Upstream ferry across a river

downstream ferry except for the different direction of the canoe. To backferry, both paddlers will have to use effective backstrokes to hold the canoe in place in the moving current. (This might be a good time to review your backstroke technique from Chapter 3. Focus on using your back to get power in your backstroke, and keep that paddle vertical during the stroke.) Now the bow paddler becomes the "stern" for purposes of setting and holding the backferry angle. You'll find it easiest for the bow to be paddling on the upstream side and the stern on the downstream side. Here's a case in which the bow paddler will call the switches if any are to be made; just make sure they're over the shoulder and loud so your stern paddler can hear. The principles are the same—speed, angle, and lean—but because you're "backward," backferrying tends to be confusing at first. Just remember that your stern is the new "bow" and should be pointed in the direction you wish to ferry.

You can practice ferries anywhere there's moving water. Start with slow current at first. It's neat. It's fun. It will feel funny the first few times you do it because your eyes will play tricks on you. It almost makes some people light-headed the first few times they do it. But once you've mastered the upstream and downstream ferries, you've bought yourself a huge chunk of freedom on the river.

Eddy Turns

You can use variations in river currents to help you turn the canoe with surprisingly little effort. In fact, you can use the current to make a long, lean, mean touring canoe fairly dance down a twisty little stream while your clueless friends are picking themselves out of the weeds.

Poke the nose of the canoe into a part of the stream that's moving more slowly than the patch of water you're riding and see how fast the current will swing the canoe around. It's great fun, and it's your best way to stop for lunch or to scout out what's ahead on the river. Find enough current differential, such as you might find behind a big rock or on the inside of a sharp turn, and the stern paddler will feel like he or she is playing "crack the whip" on skates.

An eddy turn (Figure 8-3) has the same elements as a ferry: speed, angle, and lean. Before you get to the turn, set up your paddling sides with the bow paddling on the inside of the anticipated turn, stern paddling on the outside. Approach that slower-moving water with enough speed to move across the eddy line (separating the fast from the slow water), but not so quickly as to whip the canoe all the way

Figure 8-3: Entering an eddy

into the slow water before the current differential has time to act on the canoe. You should anticipate taking an angle to the eddyline of about forty-five to sixty degrees. Enter at ninety degrees, and the sudden change of current as you cross the eddy line may jerk your bow to the side more quickly than you can react; enter at more than ninety degrees, and you really are ferrying into the eddy, not turning.

As the bow enters quieter water in the eddy, the bow paddler plants a post (static draw) in the quiet water. Plant the paddle deep and make sure that the blade has plenty of angle. The bow paddler leans into the turn, making sure the canoe hull is leaned as well. A lot can go wrong on a snappy eddy turn, but a solid boat lean will cover a lot of sins. Hold the lean until the turn is fully complete. This, simply stated, is the way you enter an eddy. River runners call it "eddying out." You can use minor variations in current speed to assist turning on any stream. Play it just right and nobody will figure out how you're doing it!

To exit an eddy and continue downstream, enter the current with some speed, with the canoe at a forty-five-degree angle to the eddy-line. The bow paddler should be paddling on the downstream side— the side you will be turning to. Drive briskly across the eddyline, with

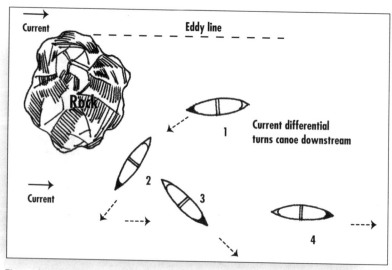

Figure 8-4: Leaving an eddy—the peel-out

Figure 8-5: Leaving an eddy using a cross-bow maneuver

the bow leaning the canoe into the turn and putting in a static draw. The boat and bow paddle will be caught by the current and the canoe will swing downstream. Once the turn is complete, reduce the lean, pour on the power, and you're on your way. You've just done a "peel-out" (Figure 8-4)!

Classical whitewater technique is a bit cleaner, and may be the only excuse for a touring paddler to learn a cross-bow maneuver (Figure 8-5), which keeps the stern paddler paddling on the inside of the turn in a better position to brace.

A word about speed, eddy turns, and canoe design. You may think you're doing the turning with your strokes, but in reality you're just helping the river; it's the *current differential* that actually turns the canoe. If you go too slowly across the eddyline you won't get the bow into the "other" water in time and you'll miss the eddy or the current. If you go too fast, you'll slice the whole canoe across the eddy line before the current differential has time to work on turning your boat. You'll become proficient at estimating how much speed is required for a particular eddyline as you practice. A longer, leaner boat takes longer to turn than a short, rockered canoe, and will need more "time" on the eddyline, which translates to less speed.

One more word about lean. Lean downstream when on a ferry.

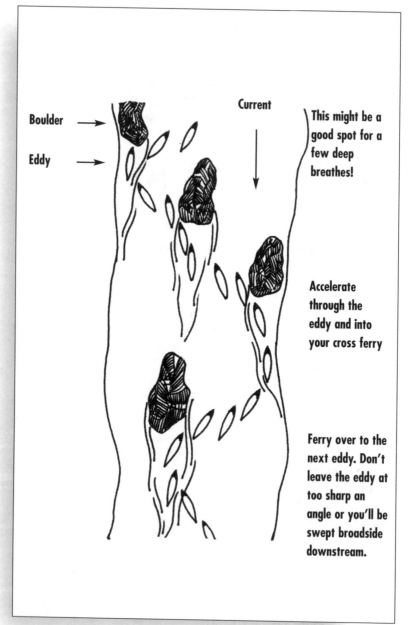

Boulder

Eddy

Current

This might be a good spot for a few deep breathes!

Accelerate through the eddy and into your cross ferry

Ferry over to the next eddy. Don't leave the eddy at too sharp an angle or you'll be swept broadside downstream.

Figure 8-6: Working upstream

Lean *into* the turn (like a bicycle cornering) when you do eddy turns. Hold the lean until the turn is complete. There, I've said it twice. If you need to hear it a third time, the river will do the talking, and when the river speaks, you get wet!

Running a Bend

Ever seen a perfectly straight river? Not likely; meanders are part of the defining character of rivers. So you're going to have to deal with bends. On any river, the current flows to the outside of a bend, and if there are trees along that outside bank, it's just a matter of time before the current erodes the bank and drops a tree into the water. The same current that cut down the tree will try to sweep you into the tree. The downed tree is called a *strainer*, and it's a good thing to encounter only if you have gills. Sometimes a tree will be hanging over the water about canoe level (a *sweeper*), and sometimes trees and debris will pile up in a *log jam*. You're going to have to find a way to run a bend that keeps you and your boat away from strainers, sweepers, and log jams on the outside of bends.

You already have one of the tools; it's the backferry. Approaching the bend in the river, begin slowing the canoe with back strokes, and set an angle with the stern of the canoe pointed to the inside of the turn. As you backferry, the current will slide you to the relative safety of the inside bank. Here's where practice pays off; you can't afford to miss on your backferry if the end result risks putting your boat into the obstruction.

There's another, more aggressive way to run a bend. As you approach the bend, begin to point the bow of the canoe toward the inside of the bend. As you continue paddling forward, keeping the bow pointed toward the inside of the bend, the river current will sweep you toward the outside of the bend, but you will power yourself away from the outside bank and any danger that it holds. It's not unlike accelerating a car out of a four wheel drift through a turn on a gravel road. The beauty of this approach is that you are setting yourself up for an eddy turn into the eddy that is always found on the inside of a river bend. If you want to stop for a break or for scouting, you're already set up; if not, scrub it off, turn downstream, and continue on.

A final, critical comment: Don't *ever* go around a bend unless you can see a clear channel continuing on downstream, or a definite place where you *know* you can stop. If you're uncertain, put the boat on the bank, get out, and take a look. River runners say it succinctly: "*When in doubt, scout.*"

Upstream Paddling

Here's where you use of lot of the strokes you've learned, and use them powerfully. And wisely, too. The upstream ferry is a necessity because you'll need to slide across the river from side to side to take the path of least resistance. High and low braces are needed because this is moving water and it exerts surprising force on your canoe. And you'd best be able to paddle forward with power, switch sides without missing a beat, and work as a team without finding fault with each other.

You don't have to be a Top Gun candidate to look at a fast-moving river and see where the slower water is. It's downstream from obstructions like logs and rocks. It's along the shoreline, more to the inside of a bend than the outside. Sometimes, if the river is fast enough, the slow-water stretches along the shoreline are actually flowing upstream. When traveling upstream (Figure 8-6), you want to seek out slow-moving water, and if you can slip your canoe into those eddies, you can catch a free upstream ride. It takes boat-handling skills and experience to ferry back and forth, find an eddy here and an eddy there, muscle upstream when you have to (and you *will* have to, sooner or later), or pop into an eddy downstream from a big rock and catch a breather. It's great fun and challenging, too.

Take Out

9

I f there's a secret all paddlers share, it's this. All paddling is great paddling, and any watercourse deep enough to float a boat is great paddling water.

So, now you know something about paddling an open canoe with another person, using a style called North American Touring Technique. And I kept the promise I made at the beginning of the book—that I wouldn't use that overwrought phrase again until the last chapter.

This is it. The music ain't goin' round again, so if you want to dance, now's the time. I hope this little book tempts you to dance with your partner in a canoe. I hope it gets you so stoked on paddling that you get off your patio furniture and spend those magical twilight hours on some local waterway every night. I hope it gets you so revved up that you try other kinds of canoeing and other kinds of canoes. They're there: maneuverable little sport tandems, incredibly responsive whitewater boats, big trippers that can swallow a month's worth of gear, and lean, mean, racing machines. They're there for solo paddlers, too. It doesn't matter what you like to do; the boats are there to do it.

And I hope you don't neglect kayaks, either. They also come in all sizes and shapes, from long, lean sea tourers to nimble whitewater play boats and those incredible little craft called squirt boats that are as at home under the water as on the surface. Now *that's* talking new dimensions in paddling!

And, when you're zipping around on the water somewhere,

feeling your muscles working, hearing a good hull carving through the water like the sound of rending silk, sensing and delighting in the skill of your partner, caressing the shaft and the grip of your paddle as you drive into it, let the boat glide for a bit. Let the birds come back to the forest canopy. Watch the slantwise sunlight flicker on the ripples of your passing. Feel your blood moving. Dip up a handful of water and splash it on your face; enjoy the tiny chill it brings. Celebrate sensation. Celebrate living. Celebrate the movement of the boat.

Because it is said that only those who move will die. But paddlers know that those who do not move are already dead.

Index

About the Author and Editor

Author Harry Roberts was the editor of *Canoesport Journal* and an avid outdoorsman, canoeist, hiker and camper.

Steve Salins' paddles have cover many miles in canoes and kayaks of all types, from whitewater to marathon canoe racing. An instructor for Pacific Water Sports in Seattle and a canoe technique columnist for *Canoe & Kayak* magazine, Steve combines an analytical, orderly, and direct style with an unbridled passion for canoeing.